Teaching Handbook for
Imperial China

Josh Brooman

LONGMAN

Longman Group UK Limited
Longman House, Burnt Mill, Harlow Essex,
CM20 2JE, England and Associated Companies
throughout the World.

First published 1992
ISBN   0 582 10170 0

Set in 11/15 pt Bodoni
Printed in Great Britain by
Longman York Publishing Services

The publisher's policy is to use paper
manufactured from sustainable forests

Designed by: Roger Walton Studio

Aunt Yi's Pancreas, page 25, is based
upon Collier Encyclopaedia vol. 6,
p335, Macmillan, 1987.
We have attempted to trace copyright
holders of material appearing in this
book and would be grateful for any
information that would enable us to
locate any we have omitted.

Contents

1 Introduction

Imperial China was written as a basic resource for a Key Stage 3 study unit on a past non-European society. In accordance with the provisions of the 1991 Education Order for history, it aims to make demands in knowledge, understanding and skills comparable to those of a core study unit; it focusses on key historical issues, chronologically, over a long period of time; it involves study from a wide range of perspectives; it displays and questions Chinese history through a great variety of primary and secondary sources; and it gives pupils opportunities to develop knowledge, skills and understanding relevant to each Attainment Target. The book thus meets all the statutory requirements for a National Curriculum supplementary study unit for Key Stage 3. First and foremost, however, it is meant to be a coherent and approachable piece of history. Throughout the book pupils are given opportunities to use and study evidence from the period, including artefacts, pictures, written sources, and also interpretations and chronicles from later periods.

The aim of this *Handbook* is to help teachers who have chosen the subject to plan and present the study unit, and to assess their pupils' attainment in it. To this end, the Handbook contains ideas, information and suggestions on the following:

- issues arising from the National Curriculum planning requirements for category C supplementary study units;
- planning a scheme of work for a study unit on *Imperial China*;
- classroom activities and tasks;
- the historical content of the unit;
- assessment, including examples of pupils' responses to the assessment tasks in Imperial China;
- a guide to further resources.

2 General planning issues

The Education Order for history contains a number of statutory requirements which must be considered when planning a study unit on Imperial China.

Focus

The first requirement is for the unit to focus on the key historical issues concerning people of non-European background in a past society (page 48).

The focus of *Imperial China* is on the material lives, spiritual beliefs and cultural achievements of the Chinese people, set in the context of the major dynasties which ruled China from the formation of the Chinese empire in 221BC up to the Mongol conquest in the thirteenth century. The book starts with an account of the First Emperor's reign in order to introduce pupils to the nature of imperial rule, and to show them how the empire was established. The second chapter describes the major dynasties that followed his reign, and outlines the ways in which Chinese society developed under their rule. Chapter 3 is devoted to the society, material life, beliefs and artistic achievements of the Chinese, while Chapter 4 describes their scientific and technological development. The book concludes with a chapter contrasting the attitudes of Chinese and European peoples towards each other.

Perspectives

The Order stipulates that category C units in Key Stage 3 (unlike any of the other study units) must involve study from a range of perspectives: political; economic, technological and scientific; social; religious; cultural and aesthetic. The table on the next page shows how this PESC formula applies to *Imperial China*.

Historical perspectives in *Imperial China*

	Chapter 1	Chapter 2
Political	7: the First Emperor unites the states 14-15: execution of the scholars 16: death of the First Emperor	21-22: the Han dynasty 26-27: the Sui dynasty 29-30: the Tang dynasty 32-33: the Song dynasty
Economic	8: common standards 9-10: transport 13: slave labour	25: eating habits 26 and 28: building works
Technological and scientific	9-10: transport 10-12: the Great Wall	
Social	10 and 14: the law	32-33: street scene in Kaifeng
Religious		22: a Han noble's tomb 25-26: Buddhist caves
Cultural and aesthetic	8: reform of the language 17: the terracotta army	

Chapter 3	Chapter 4	Chapter 5
	60: predicting earthquakes 63: writing and government 69: the Imperial astronomer	76-77: Marco Polo and Kublai Khan
45: stir-frying		77-78: sources 9 and 10
54-55: the cycle of the years	60-61: the seismoscope 61-62: flying 62-64: paper 64-65: printing 66-67: gunpowder 68-69: clockwork	79: maps from the Catalan Atlas
36: social classes 39: housing 40: family life 41-43: women		
47-48: Daoism 49-51: Buddhism 52-54: Confucianism 56: ancestor worship 56-57: the search for immortality 58-59: Three teachings	65: the Diamond Sutra 67: Mara and demons	72: the Ebstorf map of the world
38: how people looked 39: houses 44: food and cooking 45-46: entertainment and relaxation 57: martial arts		72-74: European maps of China 74-75: Chinese maps of the West 75-76: contacts between China & West

Links with attainment targets

A general requirement of the Key Stage 3 programme of study is that every study unit must provide opportunities for pupils to develop knowledge, understanding and skills relevant to each of the attainment targets.

The content of *Imperial China* lends itself naturally to five chapters, each focussing on a different aspect of the period. Thus each chapter focusses mainly on one attainment target or strand. In particular, the Review and Assessment pages at the end of the chapters have been designed to assess pupils' knowledge and understanding of the content and the skills within the attainment target for the chapter. Questions within the narrative of a chapter both aid understanding, reinforcing concepts and ideas introduced in the text and sources, and also provide opportunities for assessment across the attainment targets. The table on page 9 shows how the book is linked to the attainment targets.

The questions within the chapter also provide starting points for pupils' own investigations. Alongside the sources, text, and illustrations they provide the stimulus and material for pupils to draw their own deductions and provide a basis to communicate their ideas in a variety of ways. The organisation and communication of historical knowledge and understanding is also a requirement of National Curriculum History for Key Stage 3. *Imperial China* offers a very different range of sources and ideas for pupils to study, increasing the breadth of the whole of their Key Stage 3 course.

Links with attainment targets in *Imperial China*

Chapter	Focus	Also contains material relevant to:
1 The First Emperor	AT2: Interpretations of history	AT1a: Change and continuity – Achievements of the First Emperor, p 7-13 – The changing map of China, pages 6 and 18 AT3: The use of historical sources – Transport, pp9-10 – The Great Wall, pp 10-12 – Execution of the scholars, pp 14-15 – The terracotta army, pp 16-17
2 The Great Dynasties	AT1a: Change and continuity	AT1b: Causes and consequences – The princess and the King of Tibet, p30 AT3: the use of historical sources – A Han noble's tomb, pp 22-23 – Buddhist caves, pp 25-26 – Was Yang Di a tyrant? pp28-29 – Street scene in Kaifeng, pp32-33
3 Life and Belief	AT1c: Knowing about and understanding key features of past situations	AT1a: Change and continuity – Lives of women at court, pp41-42 – Food and cooking, p44 AT1b: Causes and consequences – Stir-fry cooking, p45 – Buddhist beliefs, pp50-51 AT3: The use of historical sources – Pictures 1-3 as evidence of social class, pp37-38 – Picture 4 as evidence of housing, p39 – Sources 8-12 as evidence of the lives of women – Menus as evidence of cooking and diet, p44 – Picture 17 as evidence of entertainment and relaxation, p46 – Picture 21 and Daoist beliefs – Pictures 22-24 as evidence of Buddhist beliefs
4 Science and Invention	AT1b: Causes and consequences	AT1c: Key features of past situations – Uses of paper, pp62-64 – Clockwork and astronomy, pp68-69 AT3: The use of historical sources – Demons and gunpowder weapons, p67
5 China and the West	AT3: The use of historical sources	AT1a: Change and continuity – Comparison of maps 2 and 12, p72 and p79 AT1c: Key features of past situations – William of Rubruk and questions 1 and 2, p75-76

Diversity and gender

The Order stipulates (on page 34) that pupils should be taught about the social, cultural, religious and ethnic diversity of the societies studied, and about the experiences of both women and men in those societies.

Imperial China was written with both these key elements in mind. Chapter 3 is devoted to the diversity of Chinese society and culture and to the great variety of religious and spiritual belief, while Chapter 2 shows how China's ethnic diversity has much to do with the centuries-long penetration of the Chinese by the people they called 'barbarians'.

The requirement to teach pupils about the experiences of women and men presented more than the usual difficulties, for very few Chinese women's lives have been individually recorded by historians. (Even Ban Zhao, a female historian of the 1st century AD, recorded only the activities of men.) Largely, this is because all but one of the Emperors were men, who staffed their governments exclusively with men and eunuchs. As the official dynastic histories which record their reigns are the major written sources for the period, information about individual women is thus hard to find. I have been able to trace only a handful. They include the country's only female ruler, Wu Zetian (ruled 690-705AD), the poet Li Qingzhao, and a heroine of the Five Dynasties period named Hua Mulan. (The latter, however, seems to be remembered only because of an uncertainty about her gender. She was a legendary figure commemorated in an anonymous 'Song of Mulan'. According to the legend, she loved her father so much that when he was called into battle against the Tatars and was unable to go, she went in his place disguised as a man. For twelve years she served in the army as a general. Once the Tatars had been beaten she revealed her identity and went back to wearing women's clothes.)

Despite the lack of written historical evidence concerning women in Imperial China, I have tried to present this topic, wherever possible, through the experiences of both men and women. Thus, Lady Xin Zhui (page 23) was chosen to illustrate the lives of the nobility, while the daughter of Emperor Tai Zong (page 30) was chosen to illustrate the nature of dynastic rule. Women are specifically portrayed in the pictures on pages 25, 30, 37, 38, 41, 42, 43, 45. There is also a substantial section in Chapter 3 on the position of women in Imperial Chinese society.

Links with other subjects

The Order states that in each key stage pupils should have opportunities to explore links between history and other subjects. Although there is no statutory requirement to do so within each unit, the National Curriculum Council recommends teachers to identify links in their planning of each unit (page D6 and diagram 8 of History Non-Statutory Guidance).

Imperial China offers the following links:

		Page
Geography: geographical skills	The states of the world in 221BC	6-7
	Exercise on road construction	10
	Question 1 (the Qin Empire)	18
	Question 3 (changing shape of China)	35
	Maps on pages 6, 18, 24, 27, 31, 34, 72 73, 74, 79	
Mathematics: number	Question 1(d) on generations	7
	The cycle of the years	54-55
Physical education	Football	46
	Eight elegant exercises	56-57
Science: explaining how materials behave	The seismoscope	60-61
forces	Gunpowder	66-67
Religious education	Daoism	47-48
	Buddhism	49-51
	Ancestor worship	56
Technology: satisfying needs	Stir-fry cooking	45
developing ideas	Flying	61-62
	Printing	64-66
	Clockwork	68-69
English		Throughout

Links with core study units

The Order states (on page 33) that a supplementary study unit should complement or extend the core study units. A supplementary study unit on Imperial China most obviously complements Core Unit 1, The Roman Empire. The Roman and Chinese empires developed at roughly the same time and exhibited many common features, yet for much of the time were unaware of each other's existence. The contrasts between them are many and fascinating. Useful links could also be made between Imperial China and Core Unit 2, Medieval Realms. The early medieval period in Britain corresponds to the Song dynasty in China, a period of brilliant cultural, scientific and technological achievement, of major economic development, and of warfare and political change. A unit on Imperial China, studied at the end of Year 7 or early in Year 8, would therefore complement and extend the ideas, themes and concepts introduced in Core Units 1 and 2.

3 Planning the scheme of work

This section of the *Handbook* contains ideas and suggestions for planning a scheme of work on Imperial China.

The scheme of work for any study unit in history will partly be shaped by considerations that have nothing to do with the subject: for example, the amount of teaching time available; the organisation of that time in the school timetable; the school's curriculum plan for history; and the relationship of history to other humanities subjects. Inevitably, therefore, the planning ideas in this section will be more applicable in some schools than in others. It is hoped, nevertheless, that any school considering a unit on Imperial China will find at least some of them useful when constructing its own planning grid.

The scheme below starts with an introductory session which is designed to familiarise pupils with China today. The sessions which then follow are grouped into five stages, each corresponding to a chapter in *Imperial China*. Each stage, like each chapter, emphasises one attainment target or strand above the others, and culminates in a brief assessment task based on that AT. Although it is assumed that the stages would be taught consecutively as a single unit, each is, to a certain extent, free-standing. The point of this is to break down the topic into manageable chunks of several weeks each, giving pupils recognisable and achievable goals.

Introductory session

Aim: to help pupils engage with the topic by locating it in time and place.
Method: some simple familiarisation activities to do with China today.
Four activities are shown here. Any or all could be used, depending on
the time available for the session.

What do these things tell us about China today?

Show pupils a series of objects from a Chinese supermarket and
restaurant, for example: a Chinese newspaper, chopsticks, a menu,
'spirit money', incense, a porcelain bowl, noodles, rice, some spices.
Discuss what they reveal about Chinese life.

and/or

In groups, pupils write down what they already know, or think they
know, about China, on poster-size sheets of paper headed 'We know
that...', 'We think we know that....'. Then the posters are grouped
together on a display board. Hopefully, common areas of pupils'
knowledge and ignorance will become apparent.

and/or

Give pupils the quiz on page 15.

Then

Help pupils to locate China geographically by doing this map exercise
on pages 16–17.

and/or

Quiz: 'What do you know about China today?'

Tick the answers you think are right. (NB Some questions have more than one answer).

1 China is
a smaller than Britain
b about the same size as Britain
c much bigger than Britain

2 The capital of China is
a Hong Kong
b Tokyo
c Beijing

3 The Chinese unit of money is the
a Yen
b Yuan
c Rupee

4 Chinese people usually greet each other by
a shaking hands
b kissing
c hugging
d bowing
e clapping

5 Chinese houses are generally made of paper and wood in case of earthquakes:
a true?
b false?

6 Most Chinese are Communists:
a true?
b false?

7 The most common religion practised in China is
a Christianity
b Buddhism
c Islam
d Ancestor worship

8 Chinese people invented all the following except
a gunpowder
b the suspension bridge
c the computer
d spectacles
e paper money

9 The main rivers in China are
a the Yellow
b the Ganges
c the Yangzi
d the Irrawaddy

10 The most common foods in China are
a noodles
b cheese
c poultry
d rice
e fruit

11 The Chinese language is understood by more people in the world than any other language:
a true?
b false?

12 The most common drink in China is
a rice wine
b tea
c beer
d soup

13 Chinese men do not have to shave:
a true?
b false?

14 The Chinese have their own alphabet:
a true?
b false?

15 Nearly a quarter of all human beings today are Chinese:
a true?
b false?

Then

Map Exercise

Study these maps, then complete these sentences

1 China is part of the continent of ....
2 China is bigger than ....., about the same size as ......, and smaller than.......
3 Britain could be fitted into China about .. times over.
4 A plane from London to Beijing would fly over the .... desert.

5 A ship sailing from London to Hong Kong crosses the .... Sea
6 ..... countries share a border with China.
7 The train from Beijing to Shanghai crosses the .... and ....rivers
8 The Yangzi river is about .... km long
9 ......, ... and .... are Chinese seaports.
10 The most mountainous region of China is .....

China and the world

China

Land over 3,000 metres:

Main cities: ●

USSR

Manchuria

Harbin

MONGOLIA

Inner Mongolia

NORTH KOREA

AFGHANISTAN

GOBI DESERT

Yellow River

Dalian

Beijing

Xinjiang

Qingdao

YELLOW SEA

PAKISTAN

Tibet

Shang-hai

EAST CHINA SEA

Chengdu

Yangzi River

Wuhan

Changsha

NEPAL

BHUTAN

Guangzhou (Canton)

INDIA

BANGLADESH

Kunming

Hong Kong

BURMA

LAOS

THAILAND

VIETNAM

CAMBODIA

SOUTH CHINA SEA

0   250   500   750   1000   1250   1500 kilometers

Stage 1

Key themes and questions:
- How was the Chinese empire created?
- What changes did the First Emperor make in his empire?
- Was the First Emperor a tyrant?

Concepts: state; empire; tyranny.

1 **Aim:** to find out when and how the country we call China came into being.

To locate the subject in time, introduce the long time-span of Chineses history by reading the story of how Prince Zheng became First Emperor of China (page 4 of *Imperial China*). Then construct a time line to show the dynasty he founded (page 7).

2 **Aim:** To find out about the changes that the First Emperor made to China

Groups of pupils could be assigned to read about one aspect each of the changes the First Emperor made to China:
- How he united the states to make an empire (page 7)
- How he changed the language, the currency, and weights and measures (page 8)
- How he changed transport (page 9) and built a Great Wall (page 11-13)
- How he changed the law (pages 10 and 14)

Then each group explains the changes using the following method:
Group 1 appoints a spokesperson, in the guise of the First Emperor, to answer the questions put to him/her by the spokesperson of Group 2. The questions should aim to find out what changes the First Emperor made, why he made them, and with what success. The First Emperor is told what to say by the rest of the group and only he/she can speak). Then, using the same rules, Group 1 puts questions to Group 2. The process is repeated with Groups 3 and 4.

3 **Aim:** To decide whether the 'excesses' of the First Emperor outweighed his achievements.
a Display on the class notice-board six differently coloured cards, each accusing the First Emperor of one 'crime'.
b Using pages 13-18 of *Imperial China*, groups think of a defence or explanation of each 'crime' and write it onto an appropriate coloured card.
c Groups then pin each defence/explanation onto the noticeboard, alongside the matching crime, and read what other groups have put down.

d The class then discusses whether the defences/explanations they have collectively thought up excuse the First Emperor.

4 **Assessment tasks** based on AT2: Interpretations of history. Use questions on pages 18 and 19 of *Imperial China*.

Stage 2

Key themes and questions:
- What is a dynasty?
- What were the main dynasties which ruled China during this period?
- How far did China change under these dynasties?

Concepts: dynasty; government; unity; invasion.

1 **Aims:** to understand what a dynasty was; and to find out about the main changes which took place during the great dynasties of Imperial China.

a Class or group discussion: why is the (British) royal family a dynasty but my family is just a family?

b The class is divided into groups which have to find out about one dynasty each (Han, Sui, Tang and Song) from Chapter 2 of *Imperial China*. Each group shows its dynasty/period on a class timeline, then the spokesperson gives a one-minute talk which must include the words:

- The dynasty lasted .. years
- A famous emperor of the dynasty was....
- The biggest change that took place during this dynasty was...
- Other changes that took place were...

2 **Assessment tasks** on AT1(a): Change and continuity. Use activities 1 – 6 on page 35 of *Imperial China*.

Stage 3

Key themes and questions:
- How was Chinese society organised?
- How did Chinese people live?
- What were their beliefs?

Concepts: society; class; Buddhism; Daoism; Confucianism.

1 **Aims:** to understand the nature of social class in China and how it differed from present day social organisation.

Teacher exposition of the four classes of Chinese society. Then pupils study the following pictures in Imperial China and decide which class the people in each picture belonged to.

Page 15: the execution of the scholars
Page 30: Tai Zong meets an envoy from Tibet
Pages 32-33: street scene in Kaifeng
Pages 37-38: pictures 1-3
Pages 41-43: pictures 9, 10 and 12 of court ladies
Page 46: pictures 17 and 18

2 **Aim:** to find out about the everyday lives of people in Imperial China.

Make a wall display illustrating the ways in which Chinese people's everyday lives were different from lives today. Using the pictures and information in Chapter 3 of *Imperial China*, small groups of pupils make posters illustrating one each of the following aspects of everyday life:

Furniture (pictures 2, 4, 9 and 17)
Food (picture 3 on page 23, page 25, page 44)
Eating a meal (pictures 4, 16 and 17)
Cooking methods (page 45)
Clothes (Page 38 and pictures 1, 2, 3, 9, 10, 12, 17, 18)
Hair styles (Pictures 3, 9, 10, 12, 17)
Houses (Picture 18 on page 33, page 39)
Games and sport (Pictures 9 and 18 and page 47)

3 **Aim:** to find out about the main belief systems of the Chinese.
Pupils research the 'three ways' of Confucianism, Buddhism and Daoism, using pages 47-54 of Imperial China, then do the assessment tasks on pages 58-59.

Stage 4
Key themes and questions:

● What scientific and technological advances were made by the Chinese in Imperial China?
● Why were the Chinese so inventive?

1 **Aims:** to find out about some important Chinese inventions; to explain why they were invented at that time.
Groups take one of the following inventions each: the seismoscope; flying; paper; printing; gunpowder; clockwork. Using Chapter 4 of

Imperial China for information, each group must devise a 'Tomorrow's World' type of presentation, as if for the TV programme, explaining how the invention works and what it will be useful for. Groups should try to illustrate their presentations with diagrams or models.

2 **Assessment tasks** on AT1(b): Causes and consequences. Use activities 1-4 on page 70 of Imperial China.

Stage 5

Key themes and questions:
Why did European and Chinese people have such mistaken ideas about each other?

1 **Aim:** to find out what medieval Europeans and Chinese knew about each other.

a Using pages 71-74 of *Imperial China*, pupils make a list of what European map-makers knew, or thought they knew about China.

b Using the knowledge they have so far acquired about China, they show the changes that would have to be made to either source 1 or source 2 to make it a more accurate map of China. Pupils could either do their own drawing, or write a list of suggested changes.

c Use pages 74-75 of *Imperial China* to make a list of what Chinese map-makers knew, or thought they knew about the West.

2 **Aim:** to consider how attitudes towards race and nationality are formed and perpetuated.

a Study sources 5 and 6 on page 75-76 of *Imperial China*, then discuss with the class (i) why an intelligent and educated person could believe the story in source 5, (ii) why Chinese people might have found the things described in source 6 very strange.

b Read to the class some stories from the *Travels of Marco Polo* (e.g. sources 8-10 on pages 76-8 of *Imperial China*). Ask pupils to explain how the *Travels* helped to change European people's ideas about China.

c Pupils study source 12 on page 79, then discuss why the map, although based on the *Travels of Marco Polo*, still showed unlikely marvels and strange beings in the Far East.

3 **Assessment tasks** based on AT3: The use of historical sources. Use questions 1-6 on page 80 of *Imperial China*.

Answers to quiz on page 8.

1 Much bigger. Britain could be fitted into China 39 times over.
2 Beijing.
3 Yuan.
4 Hand-shaking and clapping. The Chinese never kiss in public.
5 False. This is, however, true of Japan.
6 False. About 38 million are party members – roughly one person in 30.
7 Buddhism. About 100 million Chinese are Buddhists, 20 million Muslims and 5 million Christians.
8 The computer.
9 Yellow and Yangzi.
10 Noodles and rice.
11 True. English comes second.
12 Tea and soup (especially in the form of hot water).
13 False – but they do generally have a lighter beard growth than western men, and so shave less frequently.
14 False. There is no alphabet in Chinese. Words are represented by thousands of different characters.
15 True. China's population in 1990 was estimated at 1,112 million. The world's population is estimated at 4.8 billion.

Year 7 pupils are unlikely to get more than half the answers right.

4 Notes on the historical content

The notes in this section amplify and explain some of the factual content of *Imperial China*, partly to forestall questions that pupils may ask about what they have read (e.g. Why does the Buddha have such big ears?) and partly to give teachers extra information to use in their presentations of topics.

Cover picture

This is a detail from a large silk banner painted in about 950AD, showing demons trying to disturb the meditations of the Buddha. Another detail from this painting is shown on page 67 of *Imperial China*. The mixture of fantasy and reality makes it an intriguing source. The archer mounted on an elephant is dressed and armoured in a realistic way but has six arms! We know from Marco Polo, writing three centuries later, that elephants were used in battle in the thirteenth century, but this elephant's toenails and tusks would suggest that the artist had not actually seen one.

Title and contents pages

The Chinese characters on these pages mean 'Imperial China.'

Chapter 1 The First Emperor

Page 5

China. Although the name China comes from Qin (pronounced Chin), the Chinese rarely call themselves Chinese, nor do they call their country China – possibly because they have traditionally reviled the harshness with which the First Emperor created the country. Their common name for themselves and the country is Zhong-guo (pronounced Jung gwo) – the 'Central Country'.

Generations. The First Emperor's claim that he was founding a dynasty that would last 10,000 generations was more than a little ambitious. Probably the oldest family in the world today is that of Confucius, who lived from 551 to 479 BC – i.e. 2,500 years ago. For most of that time his direct descendants lived in the same street in Qufu, his home-town, leaving only in the middle of this century during the turmoil of war and revolution. His last direct descendants are still alive and living in Nanjing and Taiwan. The youngest represents the 78th generation of the family!

Page 8

Coins from the warring states. The coin on the left is an example of 'knife money', that on bottom right is an example of 'spade money'. Generally speaking, spade money was from the central states (Hann, Zhao, Wei, Song, Yan and Chu) while knife money was used mainly in Qi. Round coins were the money of Qin. The writing on the coins shows where they were minted: a typical inscription is 'Legal money of Qi'. *The written language.* Further complications result from the fact that the Chinese language has no tenses, singulars, plurals, or definite or indefinite articles. The same word can mean several different things according to how it is spoken – in a high level, rising, low, or falling-then-rising tone. An extreme example is reproduced opposite – a story that, in writing, tells how Aunt Yi was cured of an illness, but which, when spoken, consists of only one word – *yi*, pronounced in a variety of ways. See also the example on page 41 of *Imperial China* which shows how the character for 'Woman' can mean different things according to how it is said.

Pages 11, 14, 16

Sima Qian (pronounced Soomar Chee-an) was one of the earliest and most distinguished of historians of any country. He was appointed Grand Historian (*Taishi Ling*) at the court of Emperor Han Wudi (ruled 140-87BC) but fell from favour and was imprisoned after defending the prominent general Li Ling for surrendering to the Xiongnu. He was castrated for this disloyalty to the Emperor. After release from prison, he spent ten years completing his Historical Records (*Shi Ji*), an account of 3,000 years of Chinese history, beginning in earliest times with legendary emperors. It had enormous influence on later historians by initiating the practice of relating history through the biographies of important people.

The story of Aunt Yi's Pancreas

In the story below, every word is pronounced *yi*. The tone of each *yi*
is shown: 1, high level; 2, rising; 3, low falling, then rising; 4, falling.
The story is read in columns from right to left.

3 Chinese Character	Pronun-ciation	Literal Translation Read down	2 Chinese Character	Pronun-ciation	Literal Translation Read down	1 Chinese Character	Pronun-ciation	Literal Translation Read down
胰	yi^2	pancreases	疫	yi^4	sickness	游	yi^1	Yi (by name)
醫	yi^1	to cure	姨	yi^2	Aunt's	姨	yi^2	Aunt
姨	yi^2	Aunt	疫	yi^4	sickness	悒	yi^4	(felt) depressed
亦	yi^4	how	以	yi^3	thereby	悒	yi^4	depressed
異	yi^4	wonderful	醫	yi^1	(was) cured	意	yi^4	(Her) idea (was)
已	yi^3	indeed!	姨	yi^2	Aunt	疑	yi^2	to suspect of
姨	yi^2	Aunt	怡	yi^2	(was) joyful	異	yi^4	(some) strange
以	yi^3	with	怡	yi^2	joyful	疫	yi^4	sickness
夷	yi^2	foreign	以	yi^3	(and) with	宜	yi^2	(She) should
衣	yi^1	garment	夷	yi^2	(a) foreign	詣	yi^4	visit
貽	yi^1	presented	衣	yi^1	garment	醫	yi^1	doctor
醫	yi^1	Doctor	貽	yi^2	presented	醫	yi^1	Doctor
亦	yi^4	how	醫	yi^1	Doctor	以	yi^3	took
益	yi^4	still more	噫	yi^1	Yea!	億	yi^4	100,000,000
異	yi^4	wonderful	醫	yi^1	Doctor	蟻	yi^3	ant's
已	yi^3	indeed,	以	yi^3	took	胰	yi^2	pancreases
矣	yi^3	too!	億	yi^4	100,000,000	醫	yi^1	to treat
			蟻	yi^3	ant's	姨	yi^2	Aunt's

Page 15

Execution of the scholars. Pupils may notice that picture 19 has been defaced: the First Emperor's eyes have been rubbed out as if, according to one writer, 'they were the devil's own'. The fact that someone defaced this seventeenth-century painting perhaps suggests that people still felt strongly about the execution 2,000 years after the event.

Page 16

The First Emperor's tomb. Although archaeologists have not yet found the tomb, they are searching for it very slowly. This is partly because they do not want to open the tomb, as and when they discover it, until they have the resources and technology to preserve everything they find. Chemical analysis of soil at the site where they are digging shows large amounts of mercury in the vicinity so, if Sima Qian's description of oceans of mercury is accurate, this would suggest that they are close to discovery. As and when they enter the tomb they will find, of course, that any 'everlasting lamps' went out long ago (because the flames would have used up all the air). The strings of any booby-trap crossbows would also have crumbled to dust centuries ago, so the archaeologists will be able to explore the tomb safely!

Page 16-17

The terracotta army. Chinese archaeologists have recently uncovered an even larger underground army, close to the tomb of the Western Han emperor Jingdi (reigned 157-141 BC) in Shaanxi province in central China. The army was discovered during road-making works in March 1990. Standing in 24 vaults covering an area the size of twelve football pitches are at least 40,000 warriors made of terracotta standing in battle formation. The actual number may run into hundreds of thousands once the whole site has been excavated. The figures are one-third life-size (60 cm tall). They are all naked, but textile fragments suggest that they were originally clothed in linen or gauze. They have no arms but holes in the shoulders suggest that the makers intended to attach arms at some stage. As with the First Emperor's army, the faces and heads are individually modelled. Unlike the First Emperor's army, these soldiers have weapons – swords, arrows, crossbows and spears, all one-third life size.

Chapter 2 The Great Dynasties

Page 23

The body of Lady Xin Zhui, according to one writer, was like that of a person who had died no more than a week earlier. Unlike Egyptian mummies, however, neither embalming nor mummification nor tanning had been used to preserve her body, nor had the internal organs been removed. Preservation was achieved purely and simply by keeping the tomb airtight so that the corpse was in anaerobic conditions.

The remains of various foods found in the grave included rice, wheat, millet and fruit, as well as the bones of hare, dog, chicken, sparrow, carp and bream.

The silk banner is painted with two visions of the afterlife. The lower half represents Peng Lai, the islands in the eastern seas where people lived for ever. The upper part represents paradise. Entry is via the gates guarded by two figures.

Page 30

Picture 16 was painted by Yan Liben (c600-673). The court ladies carrying the Emperor are waving fans above his head to create a cool breeze, while one carries a red parasol. Standing at attention before the Emperor are a Chinese protocol officer in red, the Tibetan envoy (called Ludongzan) in brocade, and a court attendant. Pupils might wonder why Emperor Tai Zong looks so big. It has been suggested that this was an artistic device used to show a person's importance: the larger the figure, the more important he/she was. Pupils could be asked to comment on what this tells them about the relative importance of the men and women in the picture.

Chapter 3 Life and Belief

Page 37

The bed in picture 2 could be an interesting talking point for pupils, especially the uncomfortable-looking head-rest. It was customary for Chinese people to sleep on hard surfaces – either on unsprung raised beds or on rush mats on the floor – and to use head-rests made of hard materials such as wood or glazed pottery. It is a good example of how the experience of comfort is to some extent culturally conditioned and is not just a creature instinct.

Page 38

The characters printed in red around the edge of the painting are the seals or inscriptions of the collectors who have owned the painting. Similar seals and inscriptions can be seen in the paintings on pages 30, 37, 42, and 43.

Page 40

Family names. Despite the huge number of Chinese people, there were only several hundred surnames. The Chinese traditionally called themselves 'the old hundred names', the commonest being Chang, Wang and Li. Variety came in their personal names. First there was the name given at birth by parents. (Boys' names often reflected their parents' hopes or ambitions – e.g. 'Great Talent', 'Victorious', 'Brave', 'Examination Success,' while girls were generally named after fruits, flowers or jewels.) Then came the 'style', or nickname which people could adopt on becoming adult, and which they chose for themselves. Below is an example of how a Chinese name is structured:

Zhou Enlai

Surname   Grace, or Favour to come

His style was Shao-shan, meaning Small Mountain

Page 41

Characters. In addition to the character for 'woman' pupils may also be interested to know that the character for father is – formed by a hand holding a stick.

Page 50

Sculptures of the Buddha. Pupils may ask why the Buddha has such big ears. Sculptures and pictures of the Buddha always show some or all of the laksana, the thirty-two major signs of perfection which distinguished the Buddha from ordinary people. These signs included a tuft of hair, or protuberance between the eyebrows (a sign of great intelligence) and elongated ears from the time when he was Prince Siddhartha and wore heavy jewelled ear-rings which distended the earlobes.

Page 52

Confucius's name in Chinese was Kong Qiu (pronounced Kong chee-oo.) He was also known as Kong Fuzi – 'Master Kong'. Jesuit missionaries to China in the seventeenth century transliterated this into a Latin form – Confucius.

Chapter 4 Science and invention

Page 60

Introduction. The list of Chinese inventions is long. In addition to those mentioned in the text were: the parachute, spectacles, underground drilling (for brine), brandy, the shoulder-harness for horses, the fishing reel, the water-mill, poison gas and the decimal point. Some inventions were later lost or forgotten. The eighth-century art of making clockwork, for example, was lost after the Mongol invasions of the twelfth century. It was then reintroduced from Europe in the nineteenth century.

Page 61

The seismoscope was another 'lost' invention. Zhang Heng's machine disappeared at some time in the third or fourth century. The picture on page 50 is a twentieth-century reconstruction, built from a detailed description of it in the *History of the Later Han Dynasty*, written in AD450. It was a seismoscope rather than a seismograph in that it showed the direction of an earthquake's epicentre but did not measure its strength. According to the History of the Later Han Dynasty there had been twenty-five major earthquakes in China since AD46. During Zhang Heng's lifetime, earthquakes rocked the capital at least six times.

Page 61-2

Flying. 'One man said he could fly a thousand li in a day' (page 61). One *li* was equal to 0.415 kilometres, so this would make an unpowered flight equivalent to the distance from Newcastle to London. As the phrase 'a thousand *li*' was often used rhetorically rather than as an accurate description of distance, this was presumably an exaggeration, to say the least.

Page 62-4

Paper. The writing on the wooden tablet (page 63) goes from top to bottom. It is thought that top-to-bottom writing developed because (a) the vertical position in which the writer held the strip, (b) the direction of the grain of the wood, and (c) the use of a soft brush for writing, made it easier to go from top to bottom than from side to side. As the (presumably right-handed) writer completed a tablet or strip, he or she would put it down with the left hand, each one successively further to the left. This explains why people later wrote on paper in vertical lines starting on the right of the page.

On the subject of toilet paper, an Arab traveller in China in AD851 wrote that 'They [the Chinese] are not careful about cleanliness, and they do not wash themselves with water after they have done their necessities; but they only wipe themselves with paper.'

The paper shoe on page 64 is very large by Chinese standards. Its present-day equivalent would be roughly a size 47 in a wide fitting. The reason for this is unknown. One possibility is that it was one of a pair of overshoes to keep a soldier's feet warm during winter on the Great Wall, where temperatures are below zero for months on end. Or perhaps they were used to make big footprints in the snow to scare Xiongnu tribesmen attempting to cross the Great Wall!

Page 64-6

Printing. 'A hand-copied book could cost anything from 40 to 5000 coins.' (page 65). It is difficult to say how much this was in today's money. As a rough guide, the average price of a kilo of grain between 100BC and AD100 was 5 coins. This would make one coin worth perhaps 10 pence in 1991 prices.

The picture on the Diamond Sutra (page 65) shows the Buddha sitting cross-legged on a throne, preaching to a monk sitting before him. The Buddha is protected by lions and fierce spirits on either side. Monks stand behind him. Note that those who are sitting do so on mats. Chairs were only just coming into use in China at this time. Note also the swastika – a holy symbol – on the Buddha's chest.

Page 66

Gunpowder. Chinese people were using fire crackers for hundreds of years before the invention of gunpowder. These were bamboo tubes sealed at both ends which exploded when thrown into a fire.

Page 68

Clockwork. The picture of Su Song's clock (page 59) is a reconstruction, based on his own written description of it. The actual tower was taken to pieces and lost by Barbarians after they captured Kaifeng in 1115.

Chapter 5 China and the West

Page 72

The Ebstorf map is one of the most famous of the medieval mappa mundi. It is a 'T-O' type of mappa mundi in which a horizontal line (representing the River Don, Sea of Azov, Black Sea, Sea of Marmora, Aegean and the Nile) and a vertical line (representing the Mediterranean Sea) form a letter T in a circular map. The writing on it is a mixture of Latin and low German, and its geographical content derives from the works of Pliny, Solinus and Isidore, as well as from imaginary accounts of Alexander the Great's campaigns. The map was preserved in a monastery in Ebstorf in Germany but was destroyed in a bombing raid in World War 2. It consisted of 30 sheets of parchment stuck together, some of which were missing when this copy of it was painted.

Page 73

The Münster map. In addition to the strange peoples pictured in the margins, the map also names the Hippophagi – a centaur-like people who were half-human and half horse.

Page 75

Strange beings who lived outside China. In addition to the strange peoples illustrated in source 4, the Shan Hai Jing mentions men with interlaced legs, long legs, long arms and giants, men with no bellies, pygmies at war with cranes, tailed men, centaurs, one-armed men, cyclops, three-headed men, three-bodied men, worms with human heads, and many more.

Page 77-8

Marco Polo's 'marvels'. Presumably the 'serpent' in source 8 was a crocodile. The burning stones in source 9 must have been coal, and the organisation in source 10 was a postal service.

Page 79

The Catalan Atlas, although incorporating Marco Polo's discoveries, still shows some unlikely marvels and strange beings. Observant pupils may be able to find a people at war with cranes, the land of Gog and Magog and a devil. More credible marvels include the pearl fishers (bottom left) and elephants.

5 Assessment

Each chapter of *Imperial China* is focussed on the attainment target that is most appropriate to its historical content. For example, one of the aims of Chapter 1 is to examine the controversial reputation of China's First Emperor. This naturally lends itself to Attainment Target 2: Interpretations of history. Similarly, one of the aims of Chapter 4 is to explain why the ancient Chinese were so inventive in science and technology: this leads naturally to questions based on Attainment Target 1(b): Causes and consequences. This is not to say that each chapter is concerned exclusively with only one attainment target. All the chapters, for example, ask questions about the use of historical sources – Attainment Target 3. And some questions, designed to provoke thought, may not relate to any of the ATs but do fulfil the requirements of historical enquiry and, importantly, reinforce the ideas and facts presented.

The tasks and questions in *Imperial China* thus fall into three categories: assessment tasks and questions on a single AT at the end of each chapter; questions covering a variety of ATs and strands, which provide assessment opportunities at intervals in the text; and questions that are intended to provoke thought rather than lead to assessment. The rest of this section is a tentative guide to some of the responses pupils might make to the assessment tasks and questions, together with an indication of the levels of attainment that such responses might suggest. These are based on trials with a group of pupils in Year 7, and the example answers include some of their responses.

Chapter 1: The First Emperor

AT 2: Interpretations of History

AT2 requires a particular contact to be set up to ask and elicit the necessary responses for each level. The selection and presentation of sources has been carefully designed to present different views of the First Emperor, his reign and achievements. The main aims of Chapter 1 are to show the many changes that took place in China during the reign of the First Emperor, and to investigate the interpretations that can be and have been made of him. Question 1 on page 18 encourages pupils to review their understanding of the changes. (It could also be used as an assessment task for AT1(a)) Question 2 assesses their ability to understand some interpretations of his reign.

The following answers indicate some likely responses and levels of attainment for questions 2 a-f:

a   Answers which identify source 24 as praising the Emperor and source 25 as criticising him, suggest level 2.

b   Answers which include an example of both a fact and an opinion, and which explain why each was chosen, suggest level 3. For example, a fact:

> The taxes were inberible. He increased the tax by thirty times bigger on salt, iron, he imposed a poll tax.

An opinion:

> People delight in his rule – scholars weren't delighted when they weren't allowed to study future or past.

c   Answers giving a plausible explanation of the difference in views might indicate level 4. For example:

> 24 was most probally written 40 years after his death because they were too scared to say it to him while he was alive and 25 was most probally written when he was alive to get on the better side of him.

d   Identification and plausible explanations of two misleading or untrue statements might indicate level 5. For example:

> There are no robbers or thieves not because there aren't any but because most are executed. Although he gave people land he took most of the profit away from the farmers.

e Pupils' completed tables might include any or all of the following:

Source 24 'He had a greedy nature' He wanted to live for ever

'He multiplied tortures' Traitors were boiled alive / torn apart by horses / cut in two / etc.

'He made punishments harsher' Wrong-doers' families had to share their punishments / robbers had their noses cut off / etc.

'The taxes were unbearable' He took as a tax half of all the food that farmers grew / he imposed a poll tax / etc.

'The Empire was crushed under forced labour' 300,000 men did forced labour on the Great Wall / thousands died making new roads / etc.

Source 25 'A new age is opened' He made China into an Empire.

'Rules and measures are corrected' He standardised weights and measures / he standardised writing / etc.

'He has made all laws clear' All Chinese people now lived by the same laws.

'Government is smoothly carried out' He divided China into 36 areas called commanderies.

'The ordinary people know peace, having laid aside their armour' He ended the wars between the warring states and took away people's weapons.

'Kinsmen help each other' Everybody was responsible for each other's good behaviour.

'There are no robbers or thieves' He sent hundreds of thousands of criminals to settle the lands outside the Empire.

Answers which select and illustrate at least three statements for each source might suggest level 6 attainment.

f Answers commenting on both views, citing examples from each, might indicate level 7.

Other assessment opportunities
Chapter 1 also contains the following assessment opportunities:

Page 7: AT 1(a): Change and continuity.
Question 1. Accurately completed time-lines, correctly showing their own lifetimes as well as the year 221BC, indicate level 2.

Pages 9-10: AT 3: The use of historical sources.
Question 2 on page 9. Plausibly explained descriptions of, e.g. a rich person or government official, suggest level 3.
Question on page 10. Convincingly drawn and labelled pictures or diagrams indicate level 4.

Page 13: AT 3: The use of historical sources.
Question 1. Answers putting together information from all four sources might suggest level 4. Answers commenting on the usefulness of some of the sources by reference to their content would indicate level 5. Answers comparing the usefulness of the sources suggest level 6.

Page 13: AT 1(c): Key features of past situations.
Question 3. Random description of the wall might indicate level 4. A description which shows understanding of how the various features of the wall relate to each other (e.g reasons for building it, location, method of building) could suggest a level 5.

Page 15: AT 3: The use of historical sources.
Question 1. Simple, basic description of what the picture shows indicates level 1. Descriptions which make deductions about the scene suggest level 3.
Questions 2 and 3. Plausible answers indicate level 4.

Page 17: AT 3: The use of historical sources.
Question 1. Plausible answers suggest level 4.
Question 2. Plausible answers suggest level 5.

Chapter 2 The Great Dynasties

AT 1(a): Change and continuity

The main aims of Chapter 2 are to introduce the main dynasties which ruled China up to the Mongol Conquest, and to give an overview of the changes which took place in China while they ruled. Questions 1-6 on page 35 assess pupils' understanding of those changes (Attainment Target 1: Change and continuity) at the same time as helping them to review what they have read in the chapter. The following are some examples of likely responses and possible levels of attainment.

1   Accurately completed time-lines would indicate level 2.
2   Lists of changes in no particular order would suggest level 3.
3   Answers which accurately identify and plausibly explain at least one aspect that changed a lot and one that did not change much would suggest level 4.

4 Tables which show examples of all the different kinds of change would suggest level 5. A table showing attainment at level 5 might include statements such as these:

	Changes in how China was governed	Changes in the economy (e.g. trade, farming, transport)
the Han dynasty	Nobbles changed to officials Chosen by public exams.	Traders from foreign countries were allowed into china.
the period of disunity	It wasn't governed Fighting always broke out between rebels.	eating rice not Wheat, more Vegetables
the Sui dynasty	There was a new law code so the government were more Strict	Built a Canal to transport grain from south to north
the Tang dynasty	Top Jobs given to officials Chosen by Public examinations	Encouraged trade With outside World.
the Song dynasty	It didn't change except for more jobs	Population went up and cities got larger. Invention of paper money helped Merchants trade more easily

5 Answers which plausibly explain a change in terms of progress/lack of progress might suggest level 6.
6 Answers which identify and explain developments that would not have happened if there had been no foreign tribes to the north would suggest level 7.

Other assessment opportunities

Page 22: AT 3: The use of historical sources.
Question 1: lists which make at least two deductions suggest level 3.
Question 2: clearly explained answers suggest level 5.
Question 3: answers which draw information from a variety of the objects, referring specifically to them, suggest level 4.

Page 28: AT 3: The use of historical sources.
Question 1: basic description of what is happening in at least one source indicates level 1.
Question 2: answers making plausible deductions about the Emperor's

Changes in religious life	Changes in Chinese culture (e.g. art, technology)	Changes in China's relations with foreign peoples
Buddist monks came to spread Buddaism	Paper, the Sun-dial and other inventions were invented	Drove away Xiongnu from it's borders
Buddhist temples built all over the country	No change Realy	China was invaded during the chaos by lots of foreign cuntries
No change (still Buddhism)		At war with Korea.
Tai Zong allowed or welcomed foreign religions into china.	Chinese pottery were very good	Relations improved as foreign traders were allowed into China
Foreign religions Continued to spread.	Became famous for art like landscape paintings.	Envaded and taken over by Mongol warriors.

power suggest level 4.

Question 3: answers which refer to the content of picture 14 might indicate level 5; and which compare picture 14 with source 12, level 6.

Question 4: answers which discuss the value and reliability of each source in turn could indicate a level 7.

Page 30: AT 1(b): Causes and consequences.

Question 1: explaining why b is the most plausible.

Question 2: answers giving one reason for the marriage might suggest level 3; two or more reasons, level 4; different kinds of reason clearly and plausibly identified, level 5.

Page 33: AT 3: The use of historical sources.

Questions 1 and 2: answers which reach plausible conclusions about China in 1100 indicate level 3.

Question 3: answers which talk about what a photograph might show indicate level 5. Answers concerning the viewpoint or intentions of the imaginary photographer might suggest level 7.

Chapter 3 Life and Belief

AT 1(c): Key features of past situations

The main aims of this chapter are to illustrate the material lives and spiritual beliefs of the Chinese people during this period. This lends itself to assessment of Attainment Target 1(c): Knowing about and understanding key features of past situations. Questions 1-6 on pages 58-59 could be used to assess pupils's knowledge and understanding of the main Chinese belief systems in their historical setting. The following are some likely responses and possible levels of attainment.

1 Answers which refer to specific differences between the pictures and another place of worship indicate level 2.

2 Answers which give a date between 528 and 479BC suggest level 3. (Pupils will need help with this exercise, for example by giving them a date chart such as the one below, and then asking them to mark on it the dates mentioned in Chapter 3 of *Imperial China*. It should then be clear when it would have been possible for the three men to meet.

	610	600	590	580	570	560	550	540	530	520	510	500	490	480	470	460	450	440
Confucius							Born 551BC. Died 479BC											
Buddha						Born 563BC, Found enlight- enment aged 35, Died 483?												
Lao Zi		according to legend, born in 604BC and lived for 160 years																

3 Answers which describe at least two differences between the three teachings might suggest level 4.

4 Plausibly explained connections between at least two of the pairs might suggest level 5.

5 Answers which describe several related reasons for becoming Buddhists might suggest level 6.

6 Answers which show clearly the connections between their beliefs and their socio-economic positions would indicate level 7.

Other assessment opportunities

Page 37: AT 3: The use of historical sources.
Correct answers would indicate a level 3.

Page 39: AT 3: The use of historical sources.
Questions 1 and 3. Answers involving straightforward deduction from the picture indicate level 3

Page 42: AT 3: The use of historical sources.
Question 1. Answers involving straightforward deduction from one or two of the sources might indicate level 3. Answers putting together information from all the sources would suggest a level 4.

Page 42: AT 1(a): Change and continuity.

Question 2(b). Answers describing straightforward changes (for example, hair styles) suggest level 3. Answers which also recognise that much did not change would indicate a level 4.

Page 44: AT 3: The use of historical sources.

Question 1. Answers to both parts of the question drawn from both menus indicate level 4. Partial answers would suggest level 3.

Page 44: AT 1(a): Change and continuity.

Question 3. Correct answers would suggest a level 2.

Question 4. Answers which suggest that cookery changed very little suggest level 4.

Page 45: AT 1(b): Causes and consequences.

Question 5. Answers showing the correct sequence of events (b, c, f, e, a, d, g) suggest level 4.

Question 6. Plausibly argued answers suggest level 6.

Page 46: AT 3: The use of historical sources.

Question 2. Answers based on deduction suggest level 3.

Question 1. Answers referring to the content of the picture might suggest a level 5. Answers referring to the specific circumstances in which the picture was produced could indicate a level 7.

Page 46: AT 1(b): Causes and consequences.

Question 3. Answers identifying straightforward differences indicate level 2.

Page 49: AT 3: The use of historical sources.

Straightforward deductions from the picture suggest level 3.

Page 50: AT 1(b): Causes and consequences.

Answers suggesting one reason indicate level 3; two reasons level 4.

Page 51: AT 3: The use of historical sources.

Answers suggesting one factor indicate level 3. Answers suggesting more than one factor, based on more than one of the scenes, would suggest level 4.

Page 53: AT 2: Interpretations of history.

Question 2. Answers suggesting that the time-gap of over a thousand years means there was a lack of evidence might indicate level 4.

Page 57: AT 1(c): Key features of past situations.
Answers identifying several differences might indicate level 2.

Chapter 4 Science and Invention

AT 1(b): Causes and consequences
The main aim of this chapter is to help pupils discover why the Chinese were so inventive in science and technology, and to find out some of the results of their inventiveness. The chapter therefore lends itself naturally to assessment of Attainment Target 1(b): causes and consequences. Question 1 on page 70 helps them review the chronology of the inventions they have studied. Questions 2 – 4 assess their understanding of reasons why these things were invented at those times. The following are some likely responses and possible levels of attainment.

1   The finished time-line could look like this:

First known in China			First known in Europe
c200	First recorded use of a kite	200 BC	
		100 BC	
		1	
105	Cai Lun invents paper	100	
132	Zhang Heng invents a seismoscope		
		200	
		300	
		400	
		500	
		600	
700-750	Block printing comes into use	700	
725	Yi Xing and Liang Zen invent clockwork		
C8th	Gunpowder invented by alchemists		
856	Earliest printed book: Diamond Sutra	800	
950?	First recorded use of gunpowder weapons	900	
1041	Bi Sheng invents moveable type	1000	
		1100	
		1200	1265 First recorded use of gunpowder
			1290 First recorded use of gunpowder weapons
		1300	1300 First recorded use of clockwork
			1309 Paper first used in England
		1400	1400-1450 Block printing comes into use
			1436 Gutenberg invents moveable type
		1500	late C16th. First recorded use of a kite
		1600	
		1700	1703 De la Hautefeuille invents a seismograph
		1800	
		1900	
		2000	

2 A completed table might show any or all of the following:

	For government purposes	For religious purposes	For military purposes	For social purposes
Paper	To keep government records.	For use in religious ceremonies, e.g. as spirit money for the dead.	For use as armour.	For personal use. Decoration.
Printing	To make official forms. To print texts for government examinations	To mass-produce Buddhist prayers and sacred writings.		For leisure use e.g. playing cards.
Seismoscope	So that the govt. could take swift action to prevent rebellions after an earthquake.			
Gunpowder		For use in fireworks at religious ceremonies.	For use in bombs and guns.	
Clockwork	To help astronomers predict good ar bad fortune for the Emperor.			To help astronomers keep records of the seasons.
Kite			For sending military messages.	For leisure use.

a Tables which correctly show one reason for an invention might indicate level 3.
b Tables which correctly show two or more reasons for inventions might indicate level 4.
c Tables which correctly show at least one reason in each column (i.e show different types of reasons) suggest level 5.
3 Answers which plausibly identify and explain an order of importance might indicate level 6.
4 Answers which show an understanding of the connections between causes suggest level 7.

Other assessment opportunities
Chapter 4 also contains the following assessment opportunities:

Page 61: AT 1(b): Causes and consequences.
Question 1. Answers identifying one motive (to spy on the enemy) suggest level 3. Answers suggesting two motives (spying and the desire for prestige) indicate level 4.

Page 62: AT 1(b): Causes and consequences.
Question 1. Answers giving one cause indicate level 3; multi-causal answers, level 4. Answers identifying different types of reasons suggest level 5.

Page 64: AT 1(b): Causes and consequences.
Question 1. Monocausal answer (e.g.'he thought wood was too heavy for writing on.') suggests level 3. Multi-causal (e.g the above, plus 'he thought silk was too expensive.') indicates level 4.
Question 2. Lists which accurately identify the different kinds of uses might suggest level 5.
Question 3. Plausibly argued answers could indicate level 6.

Page 66: AT 1(b): Causes and consequences.
Question 1. Correctly arranged lists suggest level 3. Answers which suggest an alternative first event indicate level 4.

Page 67: AT 3: The use of historical sources.
Question 2. Answers, whether yes or no, which rely on a deduction from the painting indicate level 3.
Question 3. Answers which refer to the content of the painting suggest level 5. Reference to the circumstances in which the painting was produced could indicate level 7.

Page 69: AT 1: Causes and consequences.
Question 3. Monocausal answers indicate level 3, multicausal answers suggest level 4, answers distinguishing between different kinds of cause (e.g. political, scientific) indicate level 5.

Chapter 5 China and the West

AT 3: The use of historical sources
The main aim of Chapter 5 is to introduce pupils to the ways in which Chinese and European peoples formed their ideas about each other, usually at odds with reality. The topic is presented through a dozen sources, half of them visual, so the questions on page 80 provide opportunities to assess pupils' ability to handle historical sources (Attainment Target 3). The following are some likely responses and their possible levels of attainment.

1 Answers identifying at least one use of old maps indicate level 2.

2 Plausible answers referring to specific features of the map suggest level 3.

3 Answers drawing information from all three sources suggest level 4.

4 Answers commenting on the usefulness or otherwise of the maps, making specific references to their content, suggest level 5.

5 Answers comparing the usefulness of the sources, making specific reference to their content, indicate level 6.

6 Clearly and fully explained answers to all three parts of the question might indicate a level 7.

Other assessment opportunities

Chapter 5 also provides the following assessment opportunities:

AT 3: The use of historical sources.

Page 74:

Question 1 and 3. Answers referring to both maps suggest level 4.

Page 75:

Question 4. Answers referring to both sources suggest level 4.

Page 76:

Question 1. Answers illustrated by reference to the content of source 5 suggest level 5.

Question 2. Answers focussed on the circumstances in which William of Rubruk heard the story suggest level 7.

Question 3. Answers drawing on information in the source suggest level 3.

Page 78:

Questions 1-3. Plausible answers indicating deduction from the sources suggest level 3.

Question 4. Answers which refer only to the content of the sources suggest level 5; which refer to the circumstances behind the writing of the book, level 7.

Page 79:

Question 5. Answers identifing and explaining at least one difference suggest level 4.

6 Guide to pronunciation

The list below is a rough guide to the correct pronunciation of Chinese names mentioned in this book. (Names which sound as they appear are not included.)

Ban Gu	*Ban Goo*	Tai Zong	*Tie dsung*
Cai Lun	*Tseye Lun (as in rule)*	Tai Zu	*Tie dsoo*
Changan	*Chan gan*	Tang	*Tarng*
Dao	*Tow (as in cow)*	Wei Zheng	*way chong*
Daodejing	*Tow ter jing*	Wen Di	*Wen dee*
Ershi Huangdi	*Airshee hwongdee*	Wu Di	*Woo der (as in her)*
Genghis Khan	*Geng gis karn*	Wu Zetian	*Woo dzertee-en*
Ju Yuan	*Joo yerwan*	Xianyang	*Shee-en yarng*
Kublai Khan	*Koo bligh karn*	Xin Zhui	*Shin joo-ay*
Lao Zi	*low (as in cow) dzoo*	Xiongnu	*Sheeyung noo*
Liu Bang	*Lee-owe bang*	Xuan Zong	*Shwarn dsong*
Li Si	*Lee soo*	Xuan Zhang	*Shwarn jarng*
Maijishan	*My jee shan*	Yangzi	*Yang dzoo*
Mawangdui	*Mar wang dway*	Yang Di	*Yang dee*
Qin	*Chin*	Yi Xing	*Yee shing*
Sima Qian	*Soomar chee an*	Yuan	*ywon*
Shi Ji	*Shee jee*	Zhang Heng	*Jarng herng*
Shi Huangdi	*Shee hwongdee*	Zhang Qian	*Jarng chee-en*
Song	*Soong*	Zheng	*Jerng*
Sui	*Sway*	Zhong-guo	*Jung (as in lung) gwo*

7 Further resources

Books

This is not a complete bibliography but a guide to the books which I found most useful when researching *Imperial China*, and which contain material that could be used for teaching purposes.

As a non-specialist in Chinese history, my starting point was a pair of recent travel books:

Paul Theroux, *Riding the Iron Rooster: by train through China*, Penguin Books, 1989
Colin Thubron, *Behind the Wall: a journey through China*, Penguin Books, 1988

Both these entertaining, sensitive and beautifully written books helped create the sense of time and place that I needed to get an entrance into the Chinese past. Both are also full of anecdotes and stories which could interest and amuse pupils in class.

Research for *Imperial China* was done in the London Library, the Bodleian Library, Oxford, Bristol Central Library and Bristol University Library, using a wide variety of secondary sources and some primary sources in translation. By far the most useful work, to which I kept returning, was:

Joseph Needham, *Science and Civilisation in China*, Cambridge University Press, 15 volumes, 1955-1988

This colossal work which, when complete, will comprise 24 massive volumes, not only describes the development of every branch of Chinese science and technology but also explains scientific thought in the broad context of Chinese civilisation. Scholarly, minutely detailed, often arcane and mysterious, it is a work that one consults rather than reads, but, more than any other that I used, illuminates and explains the 'otherness' of Chinese civilisation. It also contains many unusual drawings, maps, diagrams and photographs.

The most useful general reference book was:
Brian Hook (Ed), *The Cambridge Encyclopaedia of China*, Cambridge University Press, 1982

Two useful general histories were:

Arthur Cotterell, China. *A Concise Cultural History*, John Murray, 1988

Bamber Gascoigne, *The Treasures and Dynasties of China*, Jonathan Cape, 1973

Books on specific topics which I found useful were:

Arthur Cotterell, *The First Emperor of China: the story of the terracotta army of Mount Li*, Penguin, 1989 – a highly illustrated and approachable account for non-specialists.

Denis Twitchett (Ed), *The Cambridge History of China*, volume 1, Cambridge University Press 1986, for the Qin and Han dynasties; and volume 3 (1979), for the Sui and Tang dynasties.

Michael Loewe, Everyday Life in Early Imperial China during the Han period, 202BC – AD220, Batsford 1968

Thomas Lawton, *Chinese Figure Painting*, Freer Gallery of Art, Smithsonian Institution, Washington D.C., 1973

Exhibitions

The most comprehensive permanent display of Chinese history in the U.K. is the T.T.Tsui Gallery of Chinese Art at the Victoria and Albert Museum in London. Although the 600 pieces on display are grouped into readily understood themes such as burial customs and everyday life, many younger pupils would probably find difficulty in appreciating them. It is perhaps an exhibition for the teacher rather than the school party. The same could be said of the Percival David Foundation of Chinese Art, Gordon Square, London, and the Chinese galleries of the British Museum.

8 About the author

Josh Brooman is a freelance writer and consultant, producing teaching and learning materials for school history. He was head of history at a comprehensive school in Croydon from 1977 until 1986, where he began writing the successful Longman Twentieth Century History Series. As a consultant for the National Curriculum Council, and member of the NCC History Group, he helped to draw up the NCC's consultation report on which the Education Order for History is based, as well as the NCC's non-statutory guidance for history.

The *Teaching Handbook for Imperial China* is a practical guide to planning and teaching the supplementary study unit Imperial China.

The *Handbook:*

shows how the pupil's book can be used in planning schemes of work which incorporate National Curriculum requirements;

suggests classroom activities based around the pupil's book;

provides additional information on the content of the unit; shows how the questions and Review and Assessment sections can be used to generate evidence of pupil attainment.

A Sense of History provides a complete package for each study unit which covers the National Curriculum content and assessment requirements, at the same time providing a history course which is investigative and fun!

LONGMAN

ISBN 0-582-10170-0

9 780582 101708